Poster Journeys

Abram Games and London Transport

For our dearest parents Abram and Marianne
with love Daniel, Sophie and Naomi

First published 2008

ISBN 978-1-85414-324-2

Published in association with the
London Transport Museum by
Capital Transport Publishing
PO Box 250, Harrow, HA3 5ZH

www.capitaltransport.com

Printed by Fabulous Printers, Singapore

Photograph on page 9 from Future Volume III No.6 1948
Special Collection Service at the University of Reading UK

Photograph of Abram Games on page 4 by Bob Barkany
Photograph on page 33 by Geoff Morant

With very special thanks to my dearest son, Theo and to my brother Daniel.
Thanks also to Jim Whiting from Capital Transport Publishing and the
London Transport Museum, who share the copyright in the published posters
with the Estate of Abram Games.

Contents

'In the early days of the war, the late Frank Pick gave a most valuable talk on poster design to the students of the Reimann school in London. His concluding words were as follows.'

" The one essential quality of a poster designer is that he should have a great variety of ideas within him. He should have great resources upon which to draw. If his range of ideas or his range of associations is small, so his posters will be poor in content. If the quality of his mind is not good, so the quality of his posters will not be good."

Austin Cooper 'Making a Poster' published by The Studio 1938

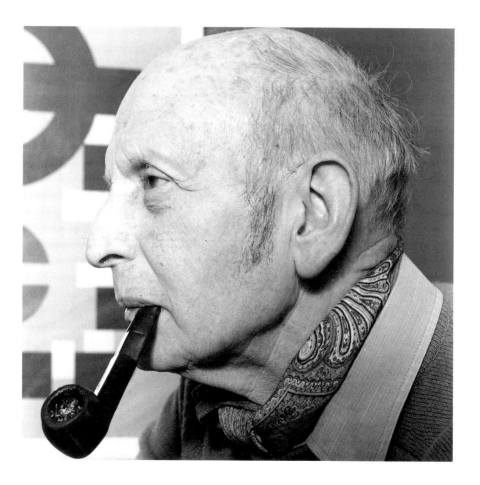

Abram Games
1990

Abram Games

"I should have paid London Transport rent. I never get disturbed on buses or tube trains; there are no visitors or telephone, but sometimes I'm so busy concentrating, I overshoot my stop."

Abram Games was a Londoner. As a young man, he took one-penny tram rides and looking from the windows, noticed the powerful London Transport and Shell posters by Edward McKnight Kauffer, Austin Cooper, Fred Taylor and Tom Purvis that adorned the hoardings. A new poster in the 1930s was an event and fresh ones appeared at regular intervals. Lines of posters formed the art gallery for the man on the street. The public took time to look, traffic was less and life was slower. Abram was determined to play a big role in British poster design. Never having had more than two terms of 'commercial art' classes, he was free of influences, free to think for himself and resolved never to be any part of such practices which seemed ethically and artistically wrong. Instead, when he began work as a designer, he devised a new form of poster for the increasingly faster and modern world. "The message must be given quickly and vividly so that the interest is subconsciously retained. Originality is secured by organising known factors in new ways. The discipline of reason conditions the expression of design. The designer constructs, winds the spring. The viewer's eye is caught and the spring is released."

Though Christian Barman was Publicity Officer at the time, Frank Pick, as Chief Executive of the London Passenger Transport Board between 1913 and 1938, would have ultimately sanctioned the twenty-three year old Games's first freelance poster commission in 1937. Pick believed the public should be encouraged to 'stretch the mind a bit more than usual'. The most important quality he expected to find in a design for a poster was directness. The only case for a 'problem poster' Abram later implied was in places like Underground trains where people had to sit idly for periods of time, and where a visual puzzle could help pass the time entertainingly. But even for a poster such as this, the whole story had to be conveyed immediately. The philosophy of maximum power of individual comment expressed in minimum terms would govern all Abram's work from now on. He called this 'maximum meaning, minimum means'.

Abram refused to drive a car. On his first and only attempt he turned it upside down. After this one lesson he was told he would be a menace to both drivers and pedestrians. He felt that if he did drive, he would lose valuable thinking time and, besides, he had little patience. Instead he travelled by public transport. He habitually sat on the top deck of London Transport buses so he could suck on his pipe. He rarely smoked it; he had problems keeping it alight, but when successful the burn holes in his sketch books, in his pockets, jumpers and trousers were numerous and legendary. He was resolute his time would never be wasted and always aimed to produce six ideas on scraps of paper before reaching the end of his journey. On every trip Abram magically produced a pencil, scraps of paper, the shopping list, an envelope, or a bill and doodled obsessively. He was training his mind to think quickly and directly on a given theme. On one such journey in 1956, sitting on top of a number two bus to Lords to watch a cricket match, he discovered he had no scraps paper to draw on. So on the back of his bus ticket, he designed his shockingly simple, five times internationally award-winning poster, the Guinness 'G'.

Abram brought the initial scribbles for a new poster back to his cold and immaculate studio in the family home. Sat at his desk, sharpened pencils lined up, he began to develop the 'thumbnails' on his layout pad. In 1990 he said "After 60 years, I still get the jitters, I am still frightened when I sit down to a new design. I'll do anything rather than start – I go for walks, read, make things, but once I have a pencil in my hand and a drawing pad in front of me, I'm lost. I never work large because my interest has always been in poster design and posters seen from a distance are small. If ideas do not work an inch high, they are never going to work." After much invited debate from his family and friends, the selected thumbnail sketch would be drawn and painted in gouache into a submission sketch – one design only would be offered to the client. If the design was rebuffed, no compromise by Abram would be made. He would politely suggest another designer be commissioned. Rejection was rare. "I am a very determined man, I will make it work if I know it's right! The success of a poster owes much to simple hard work. The gestation period of the birth of a new design can be long and agonising. There are many roughs, pain and grief before a design emerges. Finding the idea is easy, but making it work is the hard part. I am a designer who has always worked entirely alone in graphic design. I enjoy the craftsmanship, I like to make my own mistakes."

Despite his aversion to art colleges, Abram was a visiting lecturer, one day a week, in the Faculty of Design at the Royal College of Art from 1946–53. Geoffrey Ireland, a student said, "It was not so much his technique in presenting his images – airbrush and cowgum galore, but the brilliance with which he arrived at an appropriate solution – the tellingness of the image. Those pages of associated ideas that filled his sketchpads, the relentless 'don't let it beat you – you beat it' attitude was so inspiring. It was his systematic approach that impressed me most."

In 1960, Abram was commissioned to write a book that would look over his shoulder at 'work in progress'. It would display his finished designs together with the roughs and progressive sketches Abram always carefully filed away. The book was intended to be a tool for students and professionals and to show how his work was conceived and developed. It has long been out of print. The following edited extract is taken from *Over my Shoulder*, published by Studio Books.

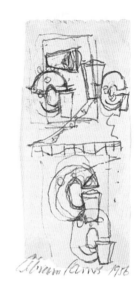

66 A design can give no more to the viewer than has been put into it by the originator. He may leave things unstated for the viewer to discover but they must first have existed in his own mind and feelings. Insincerity is soon detected, for superficiality cannot stand examination or perform any task. Design which has been deeply felt and developed, the subject of conscience and concentration, has a profundity and effect immediately recognised, respected and responded to.

When my interest in the poster was still young, I realised how this thrilling visual medium was made dull and lifeless by those who regarded it as a coloured picture with lettering imposed. It was usual at the time for 'posters' to be 'designed' without a definite subject let alone a client in mind. Appropriate lettering was added in a convenient blank space once a client could be found to buy the poster. A picture of a prepared table, for instance, might be sold and lettered for a manufacturer of furniture, foodstuffs, linen or crockery. It made no difference to the artist or seller as long as he was paid. Neither did it matter very much to the client for if he bought the drawing it was unquestionably right for him. The artists were willing accomplices in the game played by printers, artist's agents and commercial studios.

The existence of this state of affairs among professionals and students alike made a deep impression on me. I regarded it as a mockery of the great work of past Masters of the poster and at worst dishonesty. The poster should be 'tailor made' in every respect. Starting with a clear idea of its purpose it should continue the 'bespoke' theory into every detail of its conception and development. The designer should be concerned with only one client and subject. Full identification with these should be attained by logic, feeling, atmosphere and more tangible characteristics such as colour, trademark, lettering etc. All parts of the design should work together, inseparable from the whole. Lettering, in particular must work equally with the design and not merely an added afterthought. If need be, lettering alone should be the basis of the idea, text should be reduced to a minimum in order to accentuate its significance. Simplicity and power were essential but content was most important of all. Nothing must appear which did not contribute to the meaning. Pictures or patterns were not good enough, they could be ready-made. Posters should not tell a story, as was generally supposed, but make a point. The concept of 'maximum meaning, minimum means' was born in my mind and is still my guide today.

To achieve all this every design must carry an important idea or, better still, that idea must be expressed through design. Originality was not to be striven after for its own sake since it was valueless without purpose. The new approach would of itself inevitably result in fresh ideas and forms, each successive task posing new problems demanding individual solutions. In turn these would stimulate new responses in the viewer and open untrodden paths of appreciation and understanding. The aesthetic aspect would look after itself in the same way as did originality. Provided the approach was sincere and the development conscientious, design would attain a high standard, and many designs of high standard would eventually make an impact, educating the public and art buyers alike.

If the designer has no clear idea of what the client expects from his design he cannot do his job. The client must brief him with all technical data, but it is the designer's business to ask questions and add to his knowledge of the subject. When he is fully informed he can break down the problem in his own way. My own method, which began with deliberate stages of analysis, is now practically subconscious. The problem is studied from all aspects, my imagination wandering freely over the possibilities. Each thought is noted down and examined in the light of the briefing. If it is not right it is ruthlessly discarded, no idea being sacrosanct. Throwing out is more important than bringing in.

When an idea appears right it is developed by modification, amplification, simplification, with absolute flexibility. Sometimes part of another idea is added to augment it but more often it will split itself or 'slide over', a fragment being developed as more significant than the whole. The process might take minutes or days, but the idea which has to be fought for must finally look as spontaneous as the sudden one. Nothing has been said about inspiration. In my view it cannot exist for the designer although it may for the painter. The idea which seems to come effortlessly is most probably the result of subconscious thought about the problem.

The basic idea is completed and enriched by the design structure growing from it. Judgement, experience, knowledge work together to integrate the parts into a complete simple unit. The treatment might flow through many experiments and emerge as something very different from the original plan. The designer must be free to shock himself if he feels it is right for the job. It is permissible to break all the rules... but only successfully.

Until some years ago I had become known by a certain technique. *(Abram used the airbrush prolifically on his posters).* It had proved itself and was undoubtedly popular. Then, it no longer satisfied me as adequate for what I wanted to express. It had become too complex and static. Over many months a series of experiments was tried out, first on small and then larger designs. I was convinced that my doubts were justified. Simplification was not only possible but strengthened the value of the idea. Larger, simpler form and colour masses, more power for impact, a freer relaxed approach, reduction of printing costs were all part of the change which evolved. There were certainly artistic and economic risks and the new designs were controversially received by clients and colleagues alike. They could not understand why a successful technique which had worked well for years should suddenly be abandoned. The basic idea is still the root of the design, even more apparent than it was before.

My work has been called symbolic, but I regard it as integration, a combination of all parts into an inevitable whole. The parts themselves are rarely symbols but recognisable and accepted realities. Selection and unification give them their fascination. This visual shorthand has been developed over the years into a language of expression for me. I have tried to use it fully to express thoughts on subjects from culture to commerce.

Every new project is started with apprehension due to a realisation of the magnitude of the problem, its possibilities, my own responsibility for what others must see and learn and lastly the fear that I might not be able to do justice to these conditions. This I regard as a healthy sign. Were it otherwise I could not demand from myself the respect and effort which the work deserves. So much great work has been achieved by designers everywhere that the challenge to still more effort must be an incentive to us all. We badly need fine ideas, fine feelings, fine values expressed through fine design.**"**

Abram achieved his ambition and became one of Britain's finest twentieth century poster designers. He uniquely became Britain's Official War Poster Artist during the Second World War and designed 300 posters in his lifetime. His inventive and startlingly effective posters for London Transport, in particular, proved very popular with the travelling public and visitors to his beloved city.

Follow Abram's train of thought as he designs his posters. See how his interactions with London Transport's passengers provide the perfect platform for his explorations in scale, impact and coherence.

As Frank Pick said "A good poster explains itself".

Artwork terms as used by Abram Games
Progressive drawings and sketches are preliminary creative work to rough stage.
Thumbnails: miniature rough design.
Submission roughs are presented to the client, painted in gouache, approximately sized 9" x 5¾", 229mm x 146mm.
Final artwork is the finished design for reproduction.
Airbrush: A spray gun used for applying paints, inks etc with air pressure from a compressor. Originally a tool for retouching photographs, then called an aerograph.

Posters on display
1947

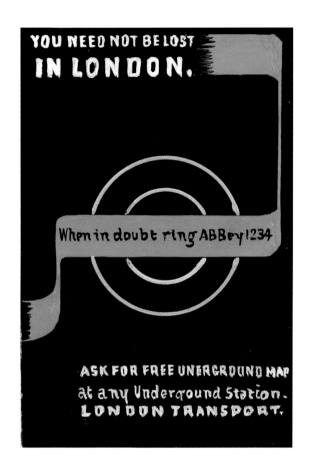

Unpublished designs
1935/6

Unpublished designs
1935/6

Concerts
unpublished poster
1936/7

Galleries
unpublished poster
1936/7

A train every
90 seconds
1937

Rough sketches showing the birth of the posters on the previous three pages.

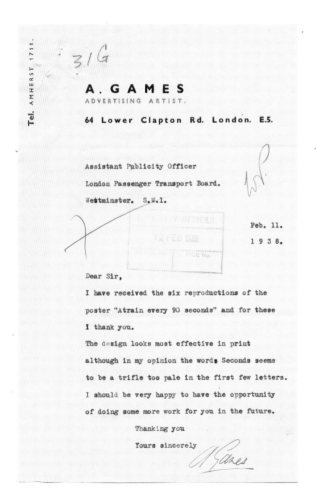

3/G

A. GAMES
ADVERTISING ARTIST.

64 Lower Clapton Rd. London. E.5.

Assistant Publicity Officer

London Passenger Transport Board.

Westminster. S.W.1.

Feb. 11.

1 9 3 8.

Dear Sir,

I have received the six reproductions of the
poster "Atrain every 90 seconds" and for these
I thank you.

The design looks most effective in print
although in my opinion the words Seconds seems
to be a trifle too pale in the first few letters.

I should be very happy to have the opportunity
of doing some more work for you in the future.

Thanking you

Yours sincerely

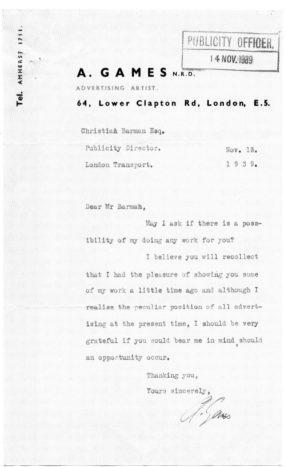

PUBLICITY OFFICER,
1 4 NOV. 1939

A. GAMES N.R.D.
ADVERTISING ARTIST.

64, Lower Clapton Rd, London, E.5.

Christian Barman Esq.

Publicity Director.

London Transport.

Nov. 13.

1 9 3 9.

Dear Mr Barman,

May I ask if there is a possibility of my doing any work for you?

I believe you will recollect
that I had the pleasure of showing you some
of my work a little time ago and although I
realise the peculiar position of all advertising at the present time, I should be very
grateful if you would bear me in mind, should
an opportunity occur.

Thanking you,

Yours sincerely,

London Transport at
London's service
1947

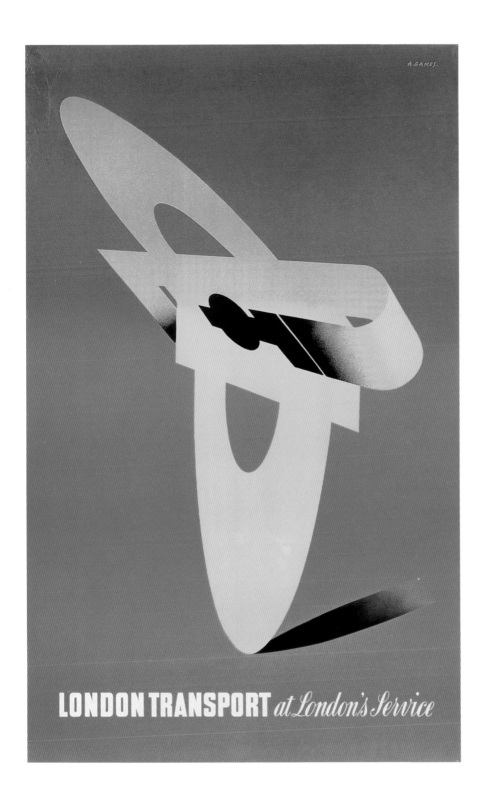

London Transport at
London's service
1947

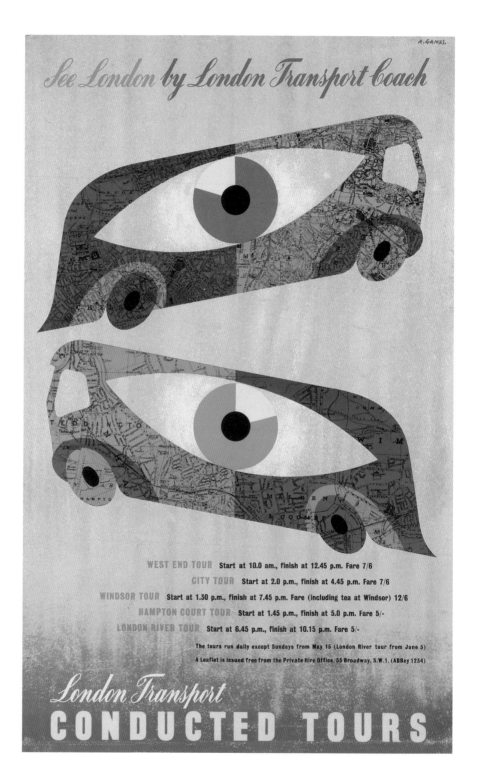

London Transport
conducted tours
1949

SEE LONDON

BY LONDON TRANSPORT COACH

1. WEST END TOUR Buckingham Palace and Changing of the Guard at Horse Guards Parade are included. It ends with a visit to Westminster Abbey. Start 10.0 a.m. Finish 12.45 p.m. **7/6**

2. CITY TOUR After a visit to St. Paul's Cathedral, the party is taken by the guide for an hour's tour of the Tower of London. Start 2.0 p.m. Finish 4.45 p.m. **7/6**

3. WINDSOR TOUR An official guide conducts passengers over the Castle, its grounds and, if open, the State Apartments. Start 1.30 p.m. Finish 7.45 p.m. (The fare including tea at Windsor) **12/6**

4. HAMPTON COURT TOUR The coach goes out through Wimbledon Common and back over Richmond Hill. Passengers may wander at will in the gardens of Hampton Court or can arrange with the guide to be taken over the State Apartments. Start 1.45 p.m. Finish 5.0 p.m. **5/-**

5. LONDON RIVER TOUR This tour of dockland includes a water-bus trip down London River through the King's Reach to the Pool of London and the Tower. Start 6.45 p.m. Finish 10.15 p.m. **5/-**

Tours 1, 2, 3 and 4 start on May 15; tour 5 starts on June 5. They run every day except Sundays, and are all accompanied by guides. All tours start at Victoria Coach Station. For further information and the reservation of seats apply to Dean & Dawson, Ltd.

81 Piccadilly, W.I   Grosvenor 3333

London Transport conducted tours
Typographical partner or 'pair poster' 1949. Harold Hutchison, Publicity Officer 1947–1966, introduced the 'pair poster' format in which a typographical partner was usually displayed alongside an illustrated poster.

London Transport
conducted tours
1950

CH

A. GAMES. F.S.I.A.

for CLAREMONT RD · SURBITON · SURREY · Elmbridge 7978

41 THE VALE · LONDON · N·W·11 · Tel· Meadway 2811

May 18. 51.

Dear Mr Hutchison,

Please have a good look at the enclosed print with the proof passed. The light green side of the buses is reading almost in reverse and is nowhere near the strength of the proof green. I feel this upsets the legibility. Mr Dean of Waterlows agrees this is a fault and suggests re-running the correct green over the existing copies. If you would agree it would help the poster enormously. The other big fault is the positioning of the word "Coach" at the top but this seems to be on the plate and could not be altered at this stage. All the same it should be put right now in case of a future run.

These two things apart Waterlows have made an excellent job of the print and I am very satisfied.

With kindest wishes,
Yours sincerely,

Abram G.

P.S. / Used you with article in 'Design'

Ref. N64   25th May, 1951

My dear Abram,

Thank you for your letter dated 18th May. I have gone into this question very carefully, and whilst it is true that on some copies the green is too light, it is also true that on other copies the green is too dark. Waterlow's admit their mistake, but unfortunately there is no possibility of re-running. I can assure you that if there was any practicable way of correcting this error we would have found it. I think you can nevertheless, be satisfied that only an expert like yourself may possibly be disappointed. The reception of the poster generally has been quite exceptional, and everybody here is delighted with it.

Kind regards.

Yours sincerely,

(HAROLD F. HUTCHISON)
PUBLICITY OFFICER

Abram Games Esq.,
41, The Vale,
N.W.11.

Printers failing to match the designer's aims are an occupational hazard. Here Abram shows understanding and appreciation of what was achieved.

Games won the
competition
to design the
Festival of Britain
emblem in 1948.
The symbol was
seen everywhere.

Festival of Britain
Information
1951

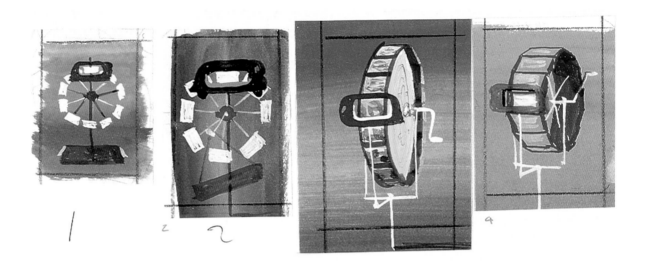

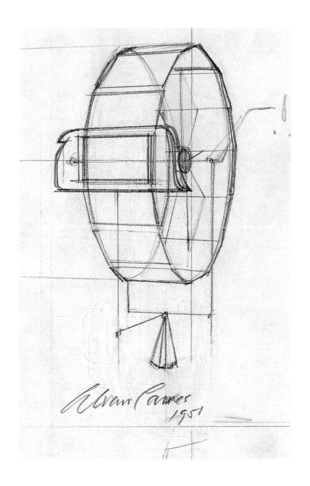

Coach and bus tours
1951

Coach and bus tours
published poster
1951

CIRCULAR BUS TOURS

CORONATION ROUTE TOUR
From May 24, a circular bus tour of the Coronation Route runs every day* of the week while the Decorations are up. Hourly buses from 10 a.m. to 10 p.m., starting at Elizabeth Bridge, off Buckingham Palace Road, S.W.1 (opposite Victoria Coach Station). Seats not bookable. Fare 1s. 6d.

CORONATION ROUTE & FLOODLIGHTING EVENING TOURS
From May 24, every evening* including Sundays, bus tours of the Coronation Route run in from 20 points in the suburbs. From June 3 tours of the Floodlit City and West End run from the same points every evening while floodlighting lasts. Coronation Route Tours start at 8 p.m., most Floodlighting Tours at 9.30 p.m. (some at 9.45 p.m.); details on local bus stop panels. Seats not bookable. Fare for all above tours 3s. 0d. From June 3 a 45-minute Floodlighting Tour also leaves Northumberland Avenue, off Trafalgar Square, each evening, including Sundays, at 10 p.m. Seats not bookable. Fare 2s. 0d.

CIRCULAR TOUR OF LONDON LANDMARKS
From May 17, every day of the week*, a circular bus tour covers 21 miles of Central London including the West End and City. Buses hourly from 10 a.m. to 6 p.m. from picking-up points in Buckingham Palace Road, S.W.1 (between Eccleston Bridge and Elizabeth Bridge); Brunswick Square, W.C.1 (near King's Cross Coach Station); Russell Square, W.C.1 (north side); and Waterloo Road, S.E.1 (outside Waterloo Station). Seats not bookable. Fare 3s. 0d. *except on June 2, Coronation Day

CONDUCTED COACH TOURS

WEST END CORONATION TOUR weekday mornings FROM JUNE 5 TO JULY 4 ONLY. Includes a visit to Westminster Abbey in its Coronation setting. 10 a.m. to 12.45 p.m. Fare 7s. 6d. (not including admission to the Abbey*)

CITY TOUR weekdays from May 11†, 2 p.m. to 4.45 p.m. Fare 8s. 6d.

RIVER & DOCKS TOUR weekdays from May 11†, 6.30 p.m. to 10.15 p.m. Fare 7s. 6d.

WINDSOR & HAMPTON COURT TOUR weekdays from May 11†, 1.30 p.m. to 7.45 p.m. Fare 12s. 6d. (including tea at Windsor)

Also on certain days of the week tours to LUTON HOO ; ST. ALBANS ABBEY & HATFIELD HOUSE ; NEWLANDS CORNER & CLANDON PARK. Fares 12s. 6d. (including tea)

Seats bookable on all Conducted Coach Tours. Apply to Private Hire Office, 55 Broadway, S.W.1 (telephone ABBey 1234), or to London Coastal Coaches Ltd., 164 Buckingham Palace Road, S.W.1 (telephone SLOane 0202), or to Dean and Dawson Ltd., 81 Piccadilly, W.1 (telephone GROsvenor 3333).

* Abbey admission : on June 5 and 6, 10/-; from June 7 to July 4, 5/- on Friday, 2/6 other days. Children, and Service personnel in uniform, half-price. †On June 2, Coronation Day, only the Windsor and Hampton Court tour will run

BUS EXCURSIONS

WHIPSNADE ZOO, WINDSOR, LONDON AIRPORT, CHESSINGTON ZOO, VIRGINIA WATER, RICHMOND and HAMPTON COURT from many parts of London, on Sundays and Bank Holidays from May 17. Seats bookable—see under Conducted Coach Tours. Return fares from 3s. 0d. to 6s. 0d.

For further information about all London Transport Tours and Excursions call on, or write to, the Public Relations Officer, 55 Broadway, S.W.1.

The photographs on the accompanying poster show (reading from top to bottom) the Gatehouse of St. Albans Abbey, St. Paul's by floodlight, the Round Tower of Windsor Castle, the Great Hall of Hampton Court Palace and Whipsnade Zoo

ST. PAUL'S CATHEDRAL · LUTON HOO · CHESSINGTON ZOO · HATFIELD HOUSE · LONDON AIRPORT · LULLINGSTONE CASTLE · CHILTERN HILLS · TOWER BRIDGE ·

SOUTHWARK CATHEDRAL · HAMPTON COURT · ST. ALBANS ABBEY · NEWLANDS CORNER · WHIPSNADE · RUNNYMEDE · LONDON DOCKS · GREENWICH PARK ·

· VIRGINIA WATER · CLANDON PARK · KEW GARDENS · ETON · SEVENOAKS · NORTH DOWNS ·

Bus and coach tours
Typographical partner
1953

Bus and coach tours
1953

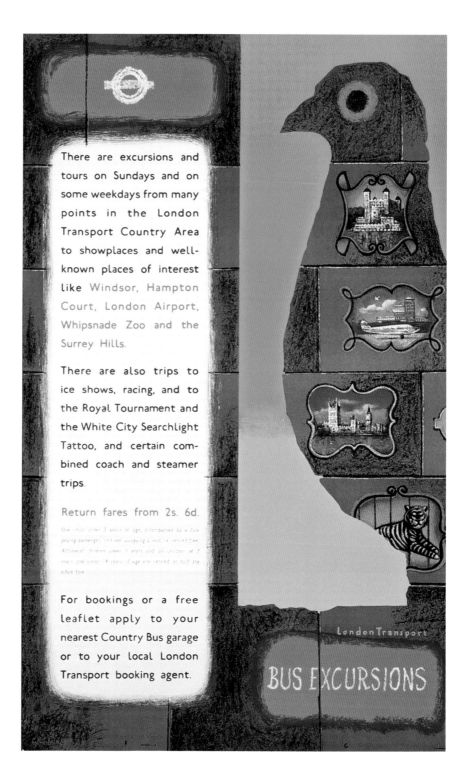

Tours and excursions
pigeon pair posters
1955

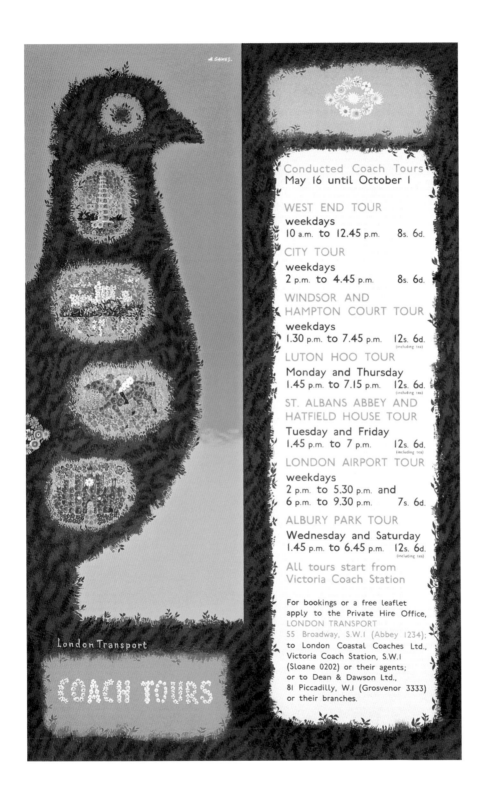

Conducted Coach Tours
May 16 until October 1

WEST END TOUR
weekdays
10 a.m. to 12.45 p.m.   8s. 6d.

CITY TOUR
weekdays
2 p.m. to 4.45 p.m.   8s. 6d.

WINDSOR AND
HAMPTON COURT TOUR
weekdays
1.30 p.m. to 7.45 p.m.   12s. 6d.
(including tea)

LUTON HOO TOUR
Monday and Thursday
1.45 p.m. to 7.15 p.m.   12s. 6d.
(including tea)

ST. ALBANS ABBEY AND
HATFIELD HOUSE TOUR
Tuesday and Friday
1.45 p.m. to 7 p.m.   12s. 6d.
(including tea)

LONDON AIRPORT TOUR
weekdays
2 p.m. to 5.30 p.m. and
6 p.m. to 9.30 p.m.   7s. 6d.

ALBURY PARK TOUR
Wednesday and Saturday
1.45 p.m. to 6.45 p.m.   12s. 6d.
(including tea)

All tours start from
Victoria Coach Station

For bookings or a free leaflet
apply to the Private Hire Office,
LONDON TRANSPORT
55 Broadway, S.W.1 (Abbey 1234);
to London Coastal Coaches Ltd.,
Victoria Coach Station, S.W.1
(Sloane 0202) or their agents;
or to Dean & Dawson Ltd.,
81 Piccadilly, W.1 (Grosvenor 3333)
or their branches.

London Transport

COACH TOURS

A.GAMES. FSIA 41 THE VALE LONDON NW11 MEADWAY 2811

Feb. 28. 57

Dear Mr Morris,

Thank you for the Rover Tickets proof. I am afraid I cannot approve the printing of the design as it now stands and would ask you whether the printer could not better it?

The background green was intended as a perfectly flat colour and the two printings now used for the grained effect should be used as flat colours for the maximum depth of colour and brilliance.

The line of white at the top of the red panel is very far from my original in weight and character.

The blue is entirely wrong and lighter in tone than the background whereas I mixed a blue with some black so as to be able to obtain it. I would say that this should not be difficult as a similar blue is now being printed on another design.

Lastly and most important the drawing of the black is unbelievably crude. It is wrong in tone and strength and wrong in its character of texture. Please compare original with it and it looks as if it had been drawn with a spade. The white register spaces on the blue bands are quite wrong and not on original. I Hope something will be done to rectify these points as at the moment the poster is being ruined on drawing alone.

Yours sincerely.

L. Morris Esq
London Transport Executive.

Rover Tickets
1956

30

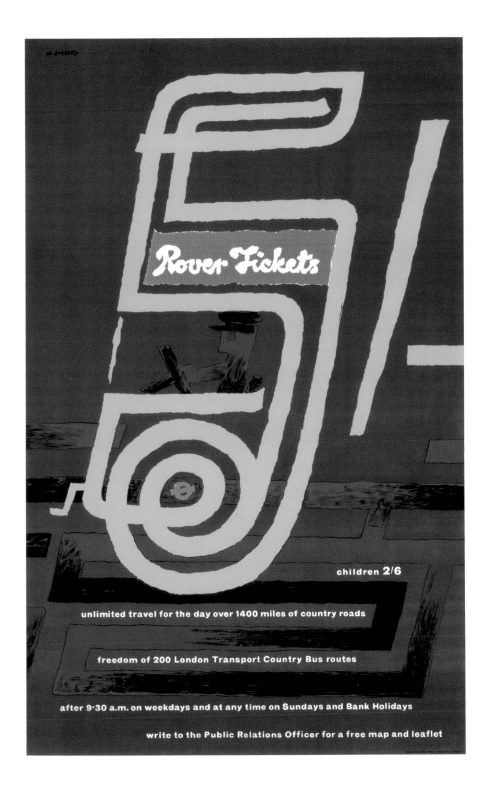

Rover Tickets
published poster
1957

   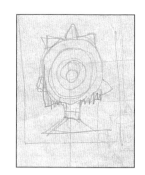

  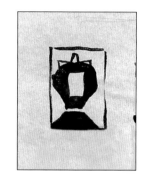 

 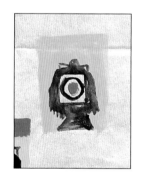  

Bus targets twins
commercial
advertising
department.
1958

London Transport conducted
coach tours
1959

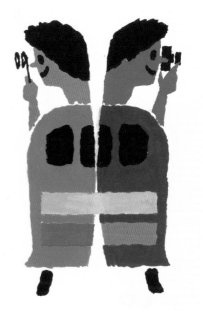

Hutchison advised Abram against
pursuing this idea – 'the backside of
a coach is not something we want
people to look at, and it is not really
worth looking at anyway,' he wrote in
September 1959.

London Transport
conducted coach tours
published poster
1960

Horse Guard
1963

Abram Games 1963

25" EXACT

Submitted Sketch.

Horse Guard
submission sketch

44

Horse Guard
published poster
1964
Unusually, there is no
obvious text in this
poster, just a small
London Transport
roundel. However.
as in many other
posters by Games,
he secreted the
names of his loved
ones within his work.
The initials of his
family are hidden
in Big Ben.

LONDON TOUR

SIGHTSEEING TOUR

Abram Games 1967

Sightsee London
1967

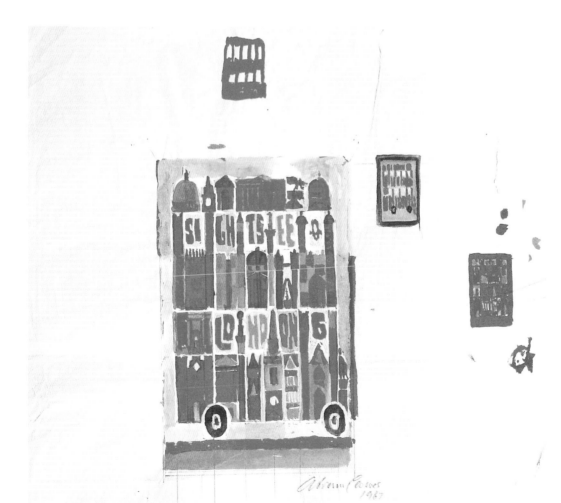

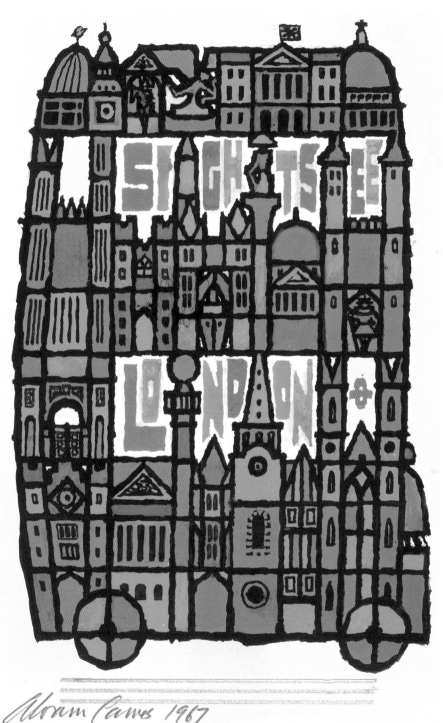

Sightsee London
submission sketch

ROUND LONDON SIGHTSEEING TOUR. Two hours, twenty miles, of the City and West End. From Buckingham Palace Road (near Victoria Station). Every day, hourly 10 00 - 16 00 (not 13 00). Fare 6/- (child 3/-). Seats not bookable.

Sightsee London
published poster
1968

Round London Sightseeing Tour
1970

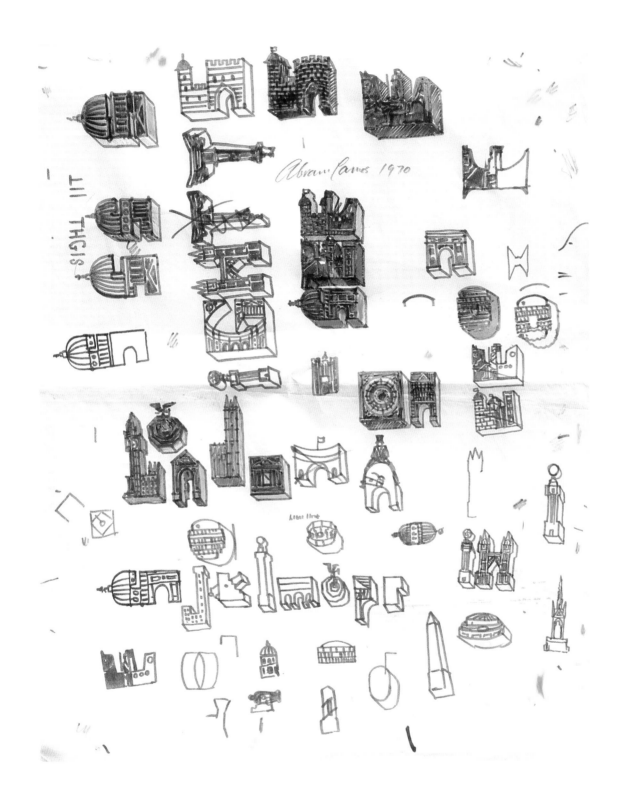

55

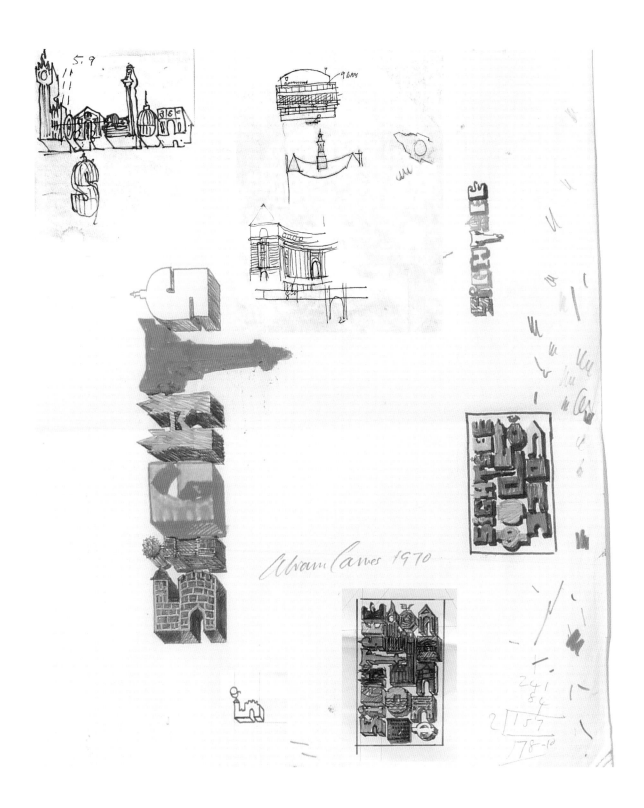

Abram Games 1970

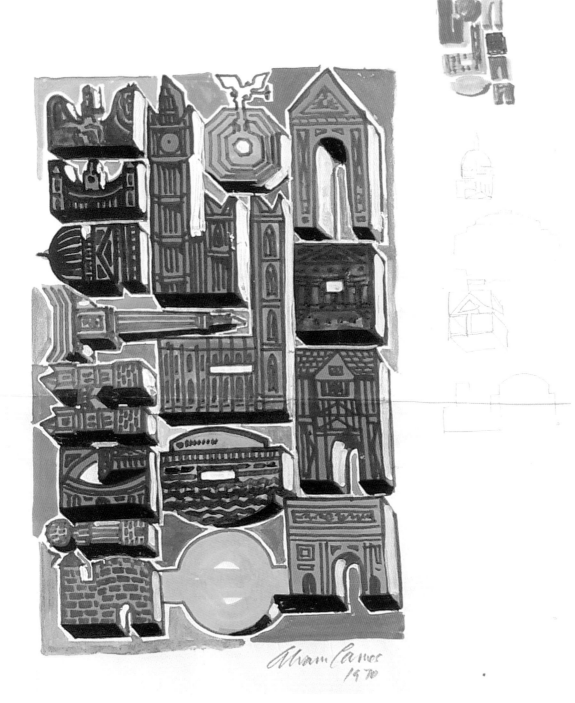

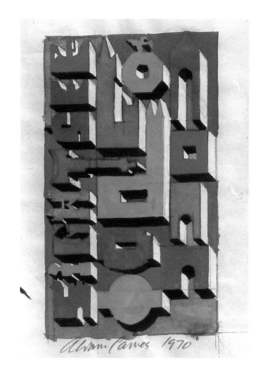

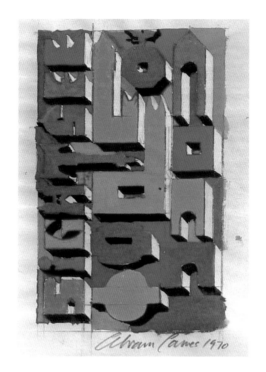

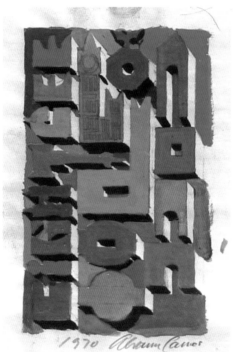

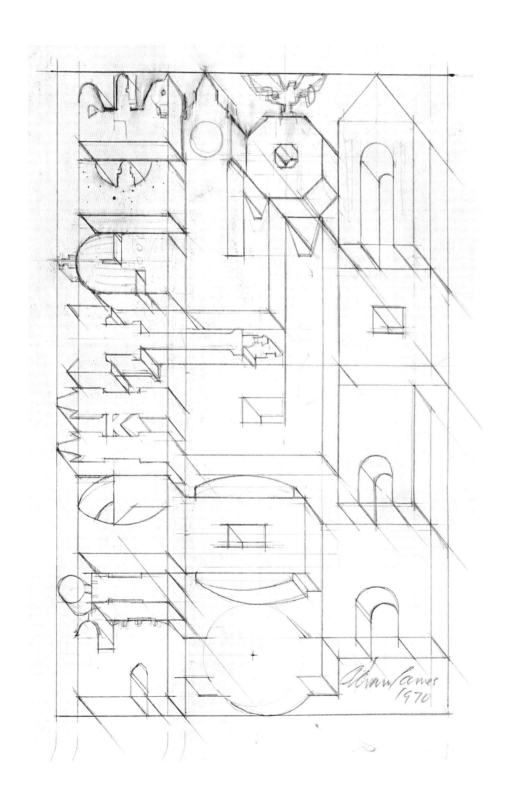

Round London
Sightseeing Tour
submission sketch

Round London
Sightseeing Tour
published poster
1971

102
843/MFL

31 October 1975

Dear Mr. Games,

This is to confirm our telephone talk when you were kind enough
to say that you would like to do a 'Zoo' poster for us, for 1976.

The text will be:

'LONDON ZOO, Regent's Park.
Go by ⊖. Underground to Baker Street, then bus 74'

We need a gay, colourful and light-hearted poster with the message
integrated with the design. I would suggest that we try not to
complicate it too much, partly because our Chairman is a great
believer in classic simplicity, and partly because, although we
fight to maintain standards, it must be admitted that, for all
the giant technical advances of recent years, one cannot always
expect the level of individual craftsmanship that we look for
granted, say, twenty years ago!

We need to show something to our masters in early January, so we
ought to have the 'Zoo' in the bag by mid-December.

Thank you for undertaking this. We very much look forward.

Yours sincerely,

M.F. Levey
ASSISTANT PUBLICITY OFFICER

A. Games, Esq., OBE, RDI, FSIA
41 The Vale
London NW11

BLP

London Zoo
1975

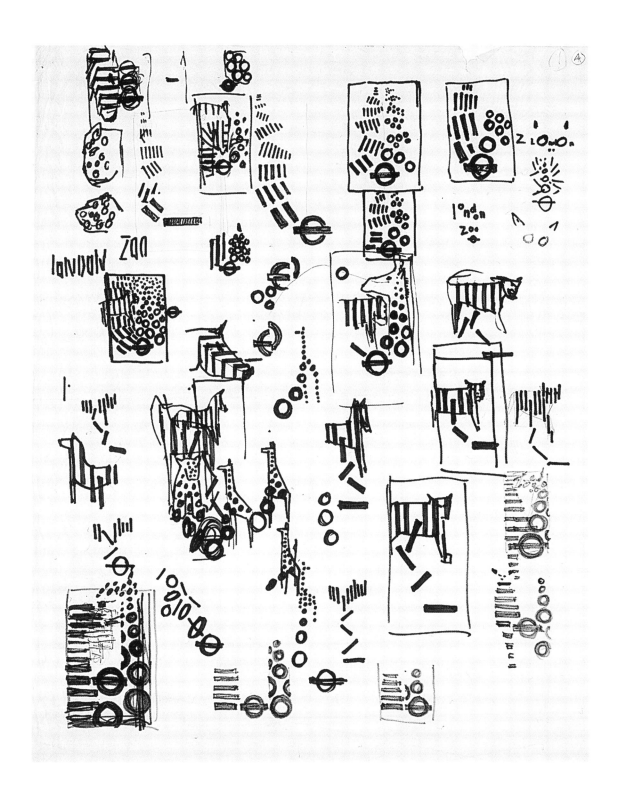

63

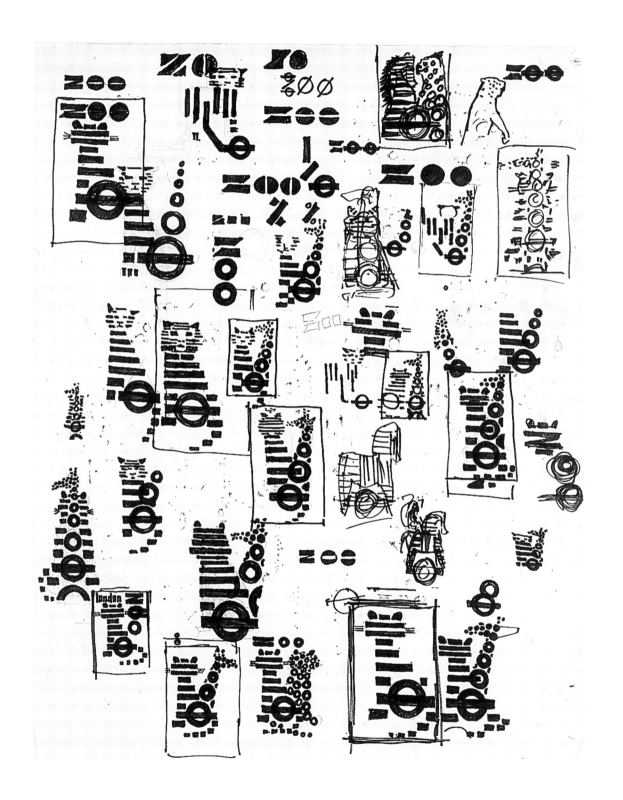

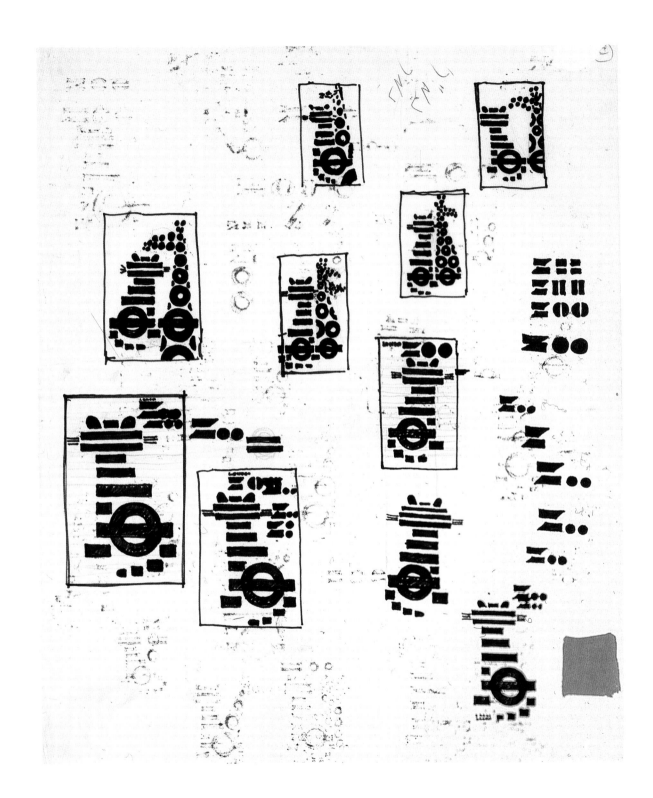

London Zoo
submission sketch

London Zoo
published poster
1975

Stockwell Swan
platform tiling
1970

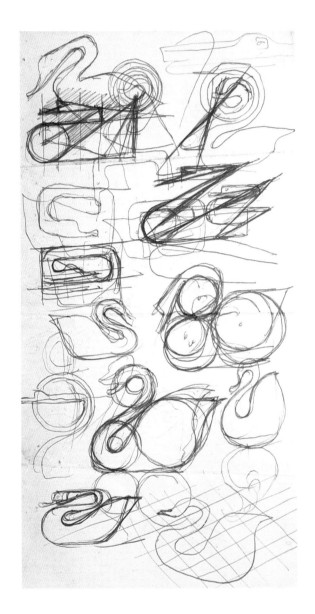

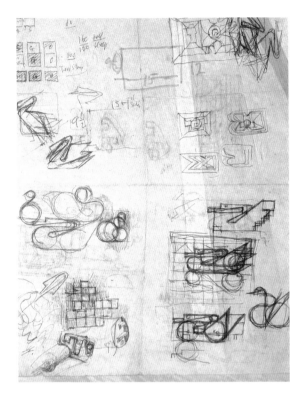

The Swan Public House in Stockwell has been in existence for centuries and a swan motif was chosen for the station on the new Victoria Line.

Abram's mind often wondered to a
copying process invention of his, as the
doodles below the swan show.

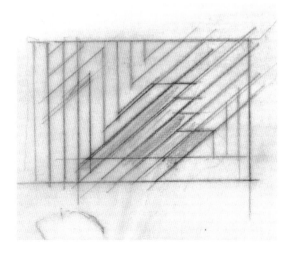

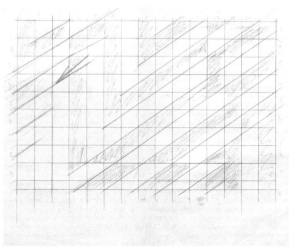

Stockwell Swan
Lithographed
tiled mural for
Victoria Line
platform seating
areas.
1970

Chronology

Abram Games OBE, RDI, Hon. D. Litt, Hon FRCA

1914
Born Abraham Gamse, 29 July in Whitechapel, London. Second son of Moshe Joseph Gamse, born 1877, photographer from Latvia and Sarah Rosenberg, born 1885, seamstress from Russo-Poland. Gamse family lived in Clapton, London E5.

1925
Left Millfields Road Primary School, Clapton, London.

1925–9
Attended Hackney Downs School, Hackney, London.

1926
Joseph Gamse changed surname to Games by deed poll.

1930
Paying student at St Martin's School of Art, London for two terms. Changed to life drawing evening classes only. Worked as assistant in father's photographic studio and prepared show cards for local tradesmen and specimens of poster designs, none accepted for publication.

1932–6
Studio boy at commercial art studio Askew Younge, Carmelite Street, London. Continued life-classes four nights weekly. Spent lunch hours studying in art galleries and Royal College of Surgeons for anatomy studies. Prepared new design specimens at home.

1935
Won second prize of three guineas in Health and Cleanliness Council poster competition. This was published as it only required two-colour printing.

1936
Won first prize of twenty pounds in London County Council Evening Class poster competition. Dismissed from Askew Younge for 'independent views'. Placed work with agents for eighteen unsuccessful months.

1937
Art and Industry published article on Games's work. After many months, obtained first poster commission from London Transport, others followed from Shell, GPO, RoSPA and industrial concerns.

1940
Called up for army service in June. Private in Royal Warwickshire Regiment, Infantry Training Battalion, Oswestry. Three months later, he was transferred to the Hertfordshire Regiment. Wrote memorandum entitled 'Army Poster Propaganda' and submitted it anonymously to the War Office.
Won second prize, Army Education Corps poster.

1941–6
January 1941, draughtsman in 54th Division Head Quarters, Moreton-in-Marsh.
June 1941 posted to War Office, London. Promoted to corporal and classified as a draughtsman in the Royal Engineers. Designed 100 wartime posters and also maps, book jackets, cap badges.

1942
Promoted to Captain and uniquely appointed Official War Poster Artist.

1945
Married Marianne Salfeld in October.

1946
Demobilised and resumed freelance design career. Rented a studio in Surbiton. Son Daniel born.

1946–53
Visiting tutor, one day a week, in Graphic Design at Royal College of Art, London.

1947
Designed stamp for 1948 London Olympic Games.

1948
May, moved to house with studio in North London.
Daughter Sophie born.
Awards:
First prize, Festival of Britain symbol, limited
competition (twelve designers).
Vienna, poster prizes:
'Post Office Greetings Telegrams', 'Radiotelegrams'.

1950
Designed the Cona coffee maker 'Rex' model.
Awards:
First prize, Independence Day stamp, Israel Philatelic
Services.
Festival of Britain Poster Exhibition, Murphy Television.

1951
Designed stamp, mural for Power and Production
Pavilion and cover for exhibition guide, Festival of
Britain, Southbank, London.
Daughter Naomi born.

1952
Awards:
First prize, BBC television moving emblem, limited
competition.
First prize Tattersall Trophy, 'Jersey Sunshade' poster.
First prize Tattersall Trophy, 'Blackpool' poster.

1953
Represented Great Britain in European poster exhibition
at Museum of Modern Art New York, (4 designers).

1956
Course teacher on Stamp Reproduction for Designers,
Philatelic Services, Israel.

1956–7
Art Director of first colour covers for Penguin Books.

1957
Awarded Order of the British Empire, OBE.
British Trade Fairs Poster Competition:
Helsinki, first prize, 'Guinness G'.

Second prize,' Jersey Umbrella'.
Third prize, 'BOAC'.
Fourth prize, 'COID' (Council of Industrial Design).
Lisbon, first prize, 'Guinness G'.

1958
Award:
Vienna, poster prize, 'Supershell ICA'.

1959
Appointed Royal Designer for Industry.
Speaker at Ninth International Design Conference,
Aspen, Colorado, USA.
Imagic copying process patented.

1960
Over My Shoulder published by Studio Books.
Awarded Society of Industrial Artist and Designers
Design Medal.
British Trade Fairs Poster Competition:
New York, first prize 'Guinness G'.
Second prize 'Jersey Deckchair'.
National Outdoor Advertising Award:
The Times Roman Bust, poster.

1961
National Outdoor Advertising Awards:
The Times Roman Bust, poster (second year).
Guinness 5 million daily, poster.

1962
Designed Cona coffee maker, table model.
Presented paper 'The Poster in Modern Advertising' to
the Royal Society of Arts.
Won the Royal Society of Arts Silver Medal.
Council of Industrial Design Poster Award:
The Times Roman Bust.
British Exhibition Poster Competition, Stockholm:
First prize, Guinness 5 million daily.
The Times Roman Bust.
British Trade Fairs Poster Competition, Stockholm:
First prize, 'Guinness G'.
Second prize, 'Jersey Deckchair'.

1963
Council of Industrial Design Poster Awards:
The Times Panto Horse.
The Times Xmas.
New York Communications Arts Award.
Jerusalem Book Fair Award:
Book cover, *Encyclopaedia Judaica*.

1964
Reduced Layer Formation copying process patented.
British Trade Fairs Poster Competition, Barcelona:
First prize 'Guinness G', no other prizes awarded.

1965
Designed Queen's Award to Industry emblem.

1965–67
Member of the Stamp Advisory Committee of the
Council of Industrial Design.

1968
United Nations Industrial Development Organisation
Consultant on Graphic Design at Bezalel School of Art,
Israel.

1970
Designed the 'Stockwell Swan' tile mural for London
Transport's Victoria Line.

1976
International Philatelic Competition for best tourists
stamps, Asiago, Italy:
First prize, Jersey set of 4.

1988
Wife, Marianne died 1 August.

1990–6
Touring exhibition '60 Years of Design'.

1991
Design and Art Direction President's Award.

1992
Honorary Fellow, Royal College of Art.

1994
Honorary Doctor of Letters, Staffordshire University.

1996
Abram Games died, London, 27 August.

Abram Games had many one-man and group
exhibitions throughout the world during his lifetime
and after. His work is in many public collections
worldwide.

For further information on the Estate of Abram Games:
www.abramgames.com

**'Abram Games, Maximum Meaning, Minimum
Means',** is a touring exhibition, available on request
from **n.games@virgin.net**.

Further reading:
Abram Games Graphic Designer
Maximum Meaning, Minimum Means
Published by Lund Humphries (UK)
ISBN: 085331 881 6

London Transport poster sizes:
All posters are double-royal size: 40" x 25",
101.6 cm x 63.5 cm except for
Festival of Britain Information 1951: 10" x 12½",
25.5cm x 31.8cm
Bus Targets 1958: double crown: 30" x 20",
76.2cm x 50.8cm
(vertical dimensions shown first)

Poster printers (with page numbers in this book)
The Baynard Press 16, 17, 23, 25, 28, 29
The Curwen Press 26, 27, 45, 61
Impress Ltd 67
Publicity Arts Ltd 33
John Swain & Son Ltd 41
Waterlow & Sons Ltd 14, 18, 19, 20, 31
The printer of the poster on page 53 is not known.